THE BRITISH TOY INDUSTRY

Kenneth D. Brown

SHIRE PUBLICATIONS

Published
Monthly

THE TOY & FANCY GOODS TRADER

Trade "
Circulation

Published in the interests of the Toy and Fancy Goods Trades

Regd. for Canadian Magazine Post.

Vol. XI.—No. 61. Annual Subscription, **5s.** post free. / Single Copies, **6d.** September, 1913.

I am the keen and happy Meccano boy. This happiness of mine is so infectious that all boys love me and smile with sheer joy when they see me. They throng round me and insist on having the use of my Meccano Outfit. This enthusiasm is a grand asset for all Toy Dealers. It means that every boy in the land will run to the shop which shows Meccano. Get a good large stock at once and be prepared for the great Meccano rush, which this year will commence earlier than usual. I will assist all dealers by advertising the wonderful merits of Meccano in the great journals and newspapers of Great Britain. Be prepared. Get your stock at once.

MECCANO

Toy dealers and stores which have handled Meccano are making "URGENT" the keynote of their orders. Meccano has created a new trade in toys. It curtails the sale of no other toys, but adds very largely to the general turnover and profits. Only those who have sold Meccano can fully appreciate its irresistible appeal to parents and children alike. Meccano presents a golden opportunity—it is for you to grasp it.

Meccano Retail Prices—Protected

Outfit No. 0 ... 3/- makes 10 models Outfit No. 3 ... 15/- makes 50 models
" No. 1 ... 5/- " 27 " " No. 4 ... 25/- " 63 "
" No. 2 ... 10/- " 41 " " No. 5 ... 55/- " 71 "
Outfit No. 6 ... 100/- makes 83 models

The Biggest Business-Puller in the Toy World

The first Meccano sale is only a forerunner of many others to follow. Boys return for additional parts and supplementary outfits. They recommend their chums to buy Meccano. So each sale represents new and continuous business. Meccano is a business creator and a profit maker. No risk; no deterioration of stock.

MECCANO Ltd
274 West Derby Rd. Liverpool

London Office and Warehouse—
5 & 6 Marshall St. Golden Square, W.

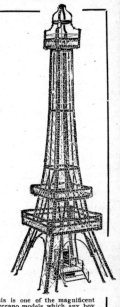

This is one of the magnificent Meccano models which any boy can build. There are hundreds of others, including Cranes, Towers, Bridges, Railways, Roundabouts and Machinery of various types. It is wonderfully simple, yet mechanically correct. Meccano consists of brightly-plated steel strips, angle brackets, plates, bolts and nuts—everything, in fact, for building the models, including tools.

THE BIRTH OF BRITISH
TOY MANUFACTURING

WRITING of his life as the child of the proprietor of a small corner shop in Salford at the beginning of the twentieth century, Robert Roberts recalled, in *A Ragged Schooling*, that while his parents never bought him toys he was quite happy with home-made ones – cottages made from gas-mantle boxes, cliffs of soda and sandy beaches composed of flour, all 'peopled with tiny figures carved from pop bottle corks'. Equally imaginative was the playground created by the writer H. G. Wells, although it comprised commercially manufactured playthings: 'many hundreds of wooden bricks … well over two hundred of lead sailors and soldiers … a clockwork crocodile of vast proportions … survivors from a Noah's Ark made a various, dangerous, albeit frequently invalid and crippled fauna … a clockwork railway … one or two clockwork boats…'. Wells's description appeared in a work of fiction, *The New Machiavelli*, but it was based on his own experiences, an accurate reflection, therefore, of the sort of toys to be found in prosperous middle-class Edwardian homes on the eve of the First World War.

As these two accounts suggest, what individual children actually had to play with was largely determined by their family's social status and prosperity, as well as their own age and gender, although many toys transcended these boundaries: books, board games and jigsaws, for example, had been produced from the mid-eighteenth century onwards, often as a sideline, by publishers, printers and mapmakers. By 1900, however, Roberts Brothers of Gloucester were well established as specialist makers of boxed games, as was Joseph Johnson, who branched out from the family stationery business by establishing the Chad Valley Company in 1897. A few years later, in 1903, washable rag books first appeared, manufactured by Dean's Rag Book Company and available in two colours for 6s. Similarly, boys and girls alike could ride in a wooden cart or on a rocking horse manufactured by Collinsons of Liverpool or by the London makers George & Joseph Lines, predecessors of the firm that would become the world's largest toy manufacturer. But such heavy wooden toys tended to be expensive and thus largely confined to professional and

Opposite: Meccano's commercial success owed much to Frank Hornby's advertising flair.

middle-class homes at a time when the average wage for an unskilled working man was about £1 a week, and for a skilled craftsman about twice that. More common and more widely distributed were wooden Noah's Arks, which for some families – mainly strict nonconformists – were still the only playthings allowable on a Sunday.

Henry Samuel Dean, founder of Dean's Rag Books.

Wooden building blocks, some illustrated with pictures or letters, and of varying shapes and sizes, provided scope for young builders. For budding artists there was modelling clay, although its utility was limited by the fact that it tended to dry out and break. From 1900, however, a more durable and colourful alternative became available in the form of Plasticine, the oil-based and somewhat smelly invention of William Harbutt.

For children whose artistic interests inclined to the theatrical, the juvenile drama remained, not as popular as in its early Victorian heyday, but kept alive largely by the endeavours of Benjamin Pollock in Hoxton. The most elaborate miniature theatres came equipped with candle-powered footlights, a safety hazard that apparently did not alarm Edwardian parents.

The workforce of G. & J. Lines, a major toy producer long before 1914.

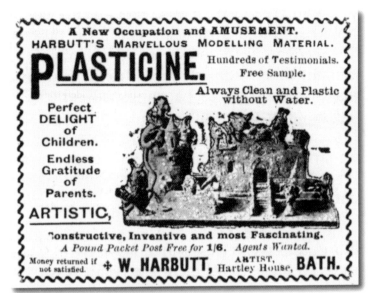

An early advertisement for William Harbutt's new modelling material, Plasticine.

A woman making dolls in her back yard, 1906. The output of individuals like her was missed in the 1907 Census of Production.

Cheap penny toys such as small squeaking animals, windmills, dolls' cutlery, whistles and tiny animals in matchboxes represented an equally dangerous fire hazard if they were made of celluloid. Fortunately for the many children whose parents could afford nothing more expensive, such toys were most commonly made of wood, paper or metal, easily put together at home by self-employed individuals. Before he found fame in the cinema, the young Charlie Chaplin was one such worker, turning out three dozen penny boats a week for an outlay of 6d.

For girls, dolls of amazingly variable qualities were available, but French and German imports tended to dominate at the more expensive end of the market. These shapely and elegantly dressed Europeans, often with glass eyes and delicate features in bisque, wax or china, looked down on their cheaper, crudely painted sisters; indeed, the most elaborate of all could close their eyes at the sight of their wooden, rag or papier-mâché inferiors. The firm of Raphael Tuck, founded by a German who moved to London in 1865, even patented a cardboard doll that could be dressed with paper clothes.

Dolls were complemented by an equally wide range of soft toys, including a relative newcomer, the golliwog, based on illustrations in a

German dolls like these were expensive and not always as prominent in British homes as is often suggested.

children's book by Florence Upton. Another new companion for British children from 1902 onwards was the teddy bear, born almost simultaneously in both the United States and Germany. Teddies were in such demand that by 1907 the German firm of Steiff, the world's leading manufacturer of high-quality soft toys, was turning out almost a million a year. The main British soft-toy manufacturer, J. K. Farnell, established in 1897, launched its own teddy-bear range in 1906, and a year later H. G. Stone established the Chiltern Toy Works, which specialised in large plush toys. Most children, however, had rather less expensive cuddly companions but, if the very cheapest had a tendency to fall apart, in the process revealing some rather unsavoury innards (soiled rags or old newspapers, for example), they could sometimes be repaired by means of a toy sewing machine, intended to encourage girls in the art of needlework.

Girls from wealthier families might also have been able to provide their dolls and soft toys with transport such as a pram or bassinet, with work in a model kitchen or shop, and even with private accommodation in the form of a wooden or tinplate dolls' house, complete with furniture and fixtures. Among these last

Early Britains' hollow-cast soldiers, mostly dating from before 1907. The smaller figures were sold singly.

9

might have been a tin teaset or stove manufactured by A. S. Cartwright, a firm of press tool makers which diversified into toys after 1905.

It was not only girls' toys that reinforced gender stereotyping. Late-nineteenth-century imperialism had strong martial overtones. Predictably, therefore, war toys remained popular among British boys in the form of weapons, elaborate military uniforms and toy soldiers, the last including the new hollow-cast variety recently invented by a London mechanical toymaker, William Britain. Their cheapness, lightness and attention to detail soon saw off their solid continental rivals made by Heyde or Mignot.

In nursery wars, young strategists could support their armies with small lead ships, representing every class of vessel in the Royal Navy (not to mention the royal yacht) and made by Bassett-Lowke, a firm of modelmakers established in Northampton at the end of the century. Boys in search of greater nautical realism could find it by deploying a model sailing boat, then much in vogue: the 1888 F. H. Ayres catalogue, for instance, offered a 29-inch yacht for 25s. For those who preferred to stick to dry land, Bassett-Lowke also designed and supplied highly detailed clockwork railway trains and vehicles, mainly made up for them by German tinplate manufacturers such as Bing, Marklin or Carette. As such,

An illustration from the Bassett-Lowke catalogue, showing the model shown at the 1908 London Exhibition.

they were beyond the pockets of most children, who had to make do at best with push-along wooden or metal railway engines.

For budding scientists there were toy microscopes and telescopes, while aspiring engineers could operate working steam engines or construct their own wooden toys using miniature tools. In 1901, however, Frank Hornby patented 'Mechanics Made Easy'. Based on perforated metal strips of varying lengths, which could be fastened together by means of standardised nuts and bolts, Hornby's invention, rebranded as 'Meccano' and extensively advertised as 'engineering in miniature', was claimed to be the world's best-selling toy by 1915. One Edwardian boy, Hubert Lansley, later wrote (in *My Meccano Days*) of his excitement as he anticipated receipt of his first set on his fifth birthday in 1912.

Lansley's set was delivered by carrier, but most toys were acquired rather more directly. Cheap toys were readily available at fairs or markets, while street vendors of these items were so numerous in parts of London that parliamentary intervention was mooted to restrict their activities. Most of the major department stores, which had became an increasingly important feature of retailing in Britain in the second half of the nineteenth century, carried toys, some on a permanent basis, others only at Christmas. The toy department in A. W. Gamage's People's Emporium stocked so

London toy hawkers in 1913.

Extract from the 1907 Census of Production, which underestimated British toy output.

TOYS AND GAMES TRADES.

TABLE I.—OUTPUT.

NOTE.—*The figures in this Table are given to the nearest thousand in each case.*

—	Great Britain.*
	£
Dolls (Rag and Dressed)	18,000
Other Toys and Games	171,000
Other Products	25,000
TOTAL VALUE OF GOODS MADE	214,000
Amount Received for Work Done for the Trade	2,000
TOTAL VALUE OF GOODS MADE AND WORK DONE.	216,000

many toy soldiers that it was popularly known as 'the Aldershot of the toy soldier world'. Many small shops also sold cheap toys as a sideline, while the very few specialist toyshops existing before 1914 usually had to sell other items as well. Wealth was still too unevenly distributed and demand too heavily concentrated in the three months prior to Christmas to support many enterprises based solely on retailing toys. Only London could sustain a dedicated toy specialist on the scale of Hamleys. Originally established in Holborn as 'Noah's Ark' by William Hamley in 1760, the firm's new Regent Street premises were refurbished at a cost of £120,000 in 1902, a well-timed decision in view of the wider variety and quantities of commercially made playthings then becoming available.

The Liverpool premises of Whiteley, Tansley & Company Ltd, an important pre-war tinplate maker.

Catering primarily for the relatively sophisticated and wealthy London market, Hamleys stocked toys of the highest quality, with many of the best lines coming from Germany – Steiff soft toys, Sonneberg dolls, bisque character dolls from Kammer and Reinhardt, Bing and Märklin

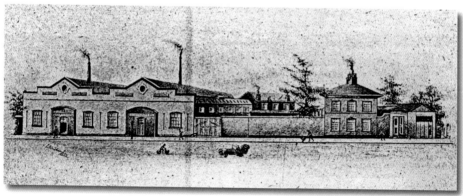

tinplate, small wooden items from the Black Forest region, and quantities of tin and lead items from Nuremberg. This served to fuel the perception, widely held by contemporaries and perpetuated ever since, that the toys of Edwardian children were almost exclusively German in origin. Germany was certainly the world's largest toy producer, and official figures show that the value of German toys exported to Britain rose by about a half between 1900 and 1914, drawn in by increases in average real incomes and reductions in the size of the British family, together with the extension of schooling and restrictions on child labour, which helped to bring about a sharper delineation of childhood as a distinctive phase in life with its own specific material needs, including playthings.

Claims of Teutonic dominance in the British nursery gained further credibility from the high profile of Germans in the distribution of toys in Britain. German names abounded among the importers and wholesalers located at the heart of the distributive network in the Houndsditch and Moorgate districts of London. The same was true in Manchester, where leading German merchant houses, who accounted for more than a fifth of all toy importers based in the city in 1913, had successfully established an annual toy fair as the most important sales event of the year.

Yet the reality was rather more complex. For one thing, claims of German pre-eminence were deliberately exaggerated by some contemporaries for political reasons, pandering to a public increasingly paranoid about the strategic threat thought to be posed to Britain by the rapid and spectacular expansion of the German economy. For another, much of the increased demand for toys in Edwardian Britain was met by a significant growth in domestic manufacturing capacity, a fact largely obscured by the first Census of Production (1907), which estimated basic British toy production at £216,000. The addition of a further £49,000 to allow for toys allocated to other categories of production was a massive underestimate of the volume of toys actually returned on schedules submitted for other trades, while the contribution of many makers was simply missed altogether. Allowing for these omissions, total British production was probably not far short of the £1 million worth of German toy goods imported in 1908. Heavy wooden and paper-based playthings had always been mainly British anyway but, contrary to popular belief, the increased quantities of innovative playthings available to Edwardian children were by no means predominantly German. They were just as likely to have been manufactured by British firms, many of them founded in the two or three decades before 1914. Many of them, like Chad Valley, Harbutt, Meccano, Farnell, Dean, Bassett-Lowke and William Britain, were destined to become household names in the course of the twentieth century.

MINIC ALL TO SCALE CLOCKWORK TOYS

Almost every type of vehicle on the road represented; **some with electric lights**. Strongly constructed, and fitted with powerful, long-running mechanism, they will run anywhere, **even on the carpet.** Disc wheels, with rubber tyres. Each model is beautifully finished in a variety of colours, and packed singly in an attractive box. Various quantities according to type are packed in strong outer fibre cases for transit.

2845 **MINIC** Light Tank. Length 3¼".

2822 **MINIC** Ford Royal Mail Van. Length 3⅜".

2821 **MINIC** Ford £100 Saloon. Length 3½".

2823 **MINIC** Ford Light Van. Length 3⅜".

2835 **MINIC** Tractor. Length 3".

2842 Vauxhall Cabriolet.

2841 Vauxhall Town Coupé.

2840 Vauxhall Tourer.

2851. Tourer with Passengers

824 **MINIC** Sports Saloon. Length 4¾".

2856 **MINIC** Mechanical Horse and Trailer with cases. Length 7¼".

2830 **MINIC** Streamline Sports. Le

2825 **MINIC** Limousine. Length 4¾".

2866 **MINIC** Double-deck 'Bus. Length 7½". Red or Green.

2826 **MINIC** Cabriolet. Length

2827 **MINIC** Town Coupé. Length 4¾".

2831 **MINIC** Learner's Car. Len

834 **MINIC** Delivery Lorry. Length 5¼".

2862 **MINIC** Single-deck 'Bus. Length 7¼". Red or Green.

2839 **MINIC** Tip Lorry. Length 5¼".

861 **MINIC** Searchlight Lorry with electric searchlight and battery. Length 5¼"

2865 **MINIC** Caravan Set (Tourer with passengers and Caravan with electric light). Overall length 9⅝".
2857 **MINIC** Caravan with electric light and battery. Length 4¼".

2860 **MINIC** Breakdown Lorry with M Crane. Length 5½".

THE INDUSTRY DEVELOPS, 1915–41

F OLLOWING the outbreak of war in August 1914 there was a predictable surge in the production of war-related toys, including weapons, board games such as the highly optimistic 'The Race to Berlin', and, in due course, tinplate tanks. Demand for toy soldiers was also high, and Britains even produced a somewhat grisly model of a trench which 'exploded' when hit in the right spot by a shell fired from a toy cannon. The Board of Trade identified toy-making as one of a number of industries which could expand in the absence of German competition, and implied that when the war ended the industry would be protected by tariffs. In response, Harwin & Company set up in 1915 as soft-toy manufacturers in the tradition of Steiff, while Dean's began to make teddy bears. Both Meccano and a new company, British Metal and Toy Manufacturers Ltd, planned tinplate clockwork train sets, while the tin-box makers Barringer, Wallis & Manners started making clockwork toys in 1914. By 1916 it was claimed that some 1,500 toy lines previously manufactured in Germany were being made by British firms.

Coupled with misconceptions about pre-war German dominance, such claims fuelled the belief, as the *Morning Post* wrote on 14 December 1931, that 'the British toy industry as we know it today may be said to date from about the beginning of 1915'. But, as we have seen, British toy manufacturing was established well before 1914, although this reality was further obscured by its gradual diversion to war work. Rising prices, shortages of skilled labour and restricted supplies of raw materials combined to make British children increasingly dependent on what smaller manufacturers, often completely new to toy-making, could knock together from whatever materials could be found. Many of the resulting playthings were of a very inferior quality and, with one or two exceptions, neither they nor their makers generally survived for very long. Thus it was generally the firms with pre-war roots that led the way forward into what proved to be something of a post-war golden age for British toys.

After 1918 a considerable investment in new plant, labour and equipment soon raised the amount of horsepower being used in British toy

Opposite:
A page from Lines Brothers' 1937–8 catalogue showing Minic model vehicles.

factories to twice its pre-war level. Thomas Salter, a London toy importer before the war, began manufacturing scientific toys in his own right in 1924. Meccano's factory in Liverpool was doubled in size, and a further 6,000 square feet was added in 1936. The previous year Chad Valley acquired an additional 20 acres. Britains opened a second factory in the 1920s and a third in the 1930s, while Dean's also moved to a large new factory. The metal-toy firm established in 1919 by Alfred Wells was so successful that it had to move to larger premises in 1921 and again in 1924. Paton Calvert Ltd, the Liverpool firm which made the Happynak range of toys, went one better, moving to bigger factories three times in the 1930s.

Most spectacular of all, however, was the development of Lines Brothers, a new enterprise established at the end of the war by the three younger sons of Joseph Lines, and which marketed its products under the brand name of Tri-ang. It grew so rapidly that within a few years it was able to build the world's most modern toy factory on a 47-acre site at Merton, just south-west of London. Heavy investment in modern equipment facilitated the mass-production of tinplate and large wheeled toys more cheaply than those made by competitors such as Patterson Edwards or Tan-Sad Ltd. Lines also turned out more expensive, high-quality versions for the top end of the market – the 1937–8 catalogue contains no fewer than eighteen types of dolls' pram – together with Pedigree soft toys, dolls, dolls' houses and model aircraft. By the early 1930s Lines Brothers had one thousand workers; five other companies employed over three hundred people, and between them British toymakers now accounted for between 60 and 70 per cent of all the toys sold in British shops, a proportion that rose to 75 per cent by the end of the decade.

This expansion of manufacturing was assisted by external events. Immediately after the war the Board of Trade denied that it had ever pledged to protect indigenous toymakers, and Britain was again opened to toy imports, although German toys initially encountered some consumer resistance. More importantly, the post-war German industry was slow to recover, dogged in the 1920s by political instability, strikes, scarcities of raw materials and hyperinflation. In the following decade it was further weakened as a number of prominent Jewish toymakers fled abroad to escape the Nazi regime. Among those who settled in Britain were F. Bing and S. Kahn, who soon joined Bassett-Lowke – for whom they

Cartoon illustrating the contemporary view that the First World War effectively created the British toy industry.

Liverpool Capturing German Trade.

A page from the 1937–8 Lines Brothers' catalogue.

had been manufacturing Trix train sets in Germany. Phillipp Ullmann and Arthur Katz, previously employed by a Nuremberg tinplate firm, established Mettoy at Northampton in 1933. A year earlier Liebetruth of Sonneberg opened a factory in London to manufacture its children's paint boxes, and about the same time another Jewish maker, J. W. Spear of Nuremberg, also established a subsidiary in Britain to make board games and activity kits.

In part, Spear's move was also an attempt to circumvent the general 10 per cent import tariff imposed in 1932 by the British government as one of a number of measures to counter the economic depression that followed the Great Crash of 1929. The major domestic symptom of the depression was, of course, mass unemployment, but it is one of the paradoxes of the

17

A delegation of British toymakers failed to persuade the Board of Trade to retain protective tariffs after 1919.

depressed 1930s that falling food prices reduced the cost of living. With average family size also still falling, many parents, the majority of whom *were* still in work, had more disposable income to spend on non-essentials. The average expenditure on toys per child in Britain rose by more than a third between 1924 and 1935, although there still remained marked regional and social variations in spending patterns.

For many less well-off parents, street markets remained important sources of toys, primarily at Christmas, allowing a father 'to get toys for his Santa Claus work ... far more cheaply than in the shops', according to M. Benedetta. But increasingly expenditure on toys *was* channelled to specialist toyshops, which enjoyed something of a boom between the world wars. More manufacturers followed Meccano's example by selling directly to retailers, so that by the 1930s only about a quarter of total retail toy sales consisted of items provided by wholesalers. With the middlemen increasingly cut out of the supply chain, toy retailing became a more attractive proposition and the number of specialist toyshops rose to almost one thousand. By 1938 they accounted for two-fifths of all expenditure on toys: departmental stores took about a third, and multiples such as the Co-operative about a quarter. Some manufacturers took their involvement with the retail sector even further. Bassett-Lowke opened its own shops in Edinburgh and Manchester. Lines Brothers, who spent the depression years buying up small manufacturers of specialised toys, also branched out into retailing by acquiring Hamleys when it collapsed in the aftermath of the Great Crash.

Hamleys was not the only casualty of inter-war economic instability: indeed, only about a fifth of the manufacturers, wholesalers and importers active in 1920 were still in business by 1940. Probably the best-known manufacturer brought down by the depression was Gray & Nicholls of Liverpool in 1930, only a few years after a journalist had described it as producing the widest range of toys in Britain. Among others which disappeared were Beddington Liddiatt Ltd and Multum in Parvo, a firm whose success with a cricket game deploying tin figures and a spring-loaded ball could not save it from liquidation in 1931. The survivors, however, included nearly all of the major pre-war manufacturers, and they were joined by some significant newcomers. Merrythought was established in 1930 to manufacture soft toys under the directorial guidance of A. C. Janisch and C. J. Rendle, recruited respectively from Farnell and Chad Valley. The first

Hamleys provided the ideal shop window for the many toys produced by Lines Brothers, new owners of the prestigious London shop from 1931.

Merrythought specialised in bears.

product listed in the catalogue was 'Greyfriars Bobby', and dogs, together with teddy bears, became a Merrythought speciality. The products sold so well that from the late 1930s the firm even emulated Steiff by inserting a pewter button in the ear of some items. Chad Valley diversified into soft toys and rag dolls. A particularly popular line was a series of velvet and felt hand-painted dolls based on characters created by the children's writer Mabel Lucie Atwell. Another Atwell character, Diddums, provided the inspiration for the first doll produced in the 1920s by a newcomer to toy manufacturing, Cascelloid. As a marketing technique, character merchandising – associating a product with a well-known figure – was nothing new to the toy industry: Jenny Lind dolls' houses had been available in the 1850s, for example. However, it derived fresh impetus between the wars from the popularity of cartoon characters made familiar to the general public by the booming cinema and press. In 1923 Dean's produced a toy based on Dismal Desmond, a cartoon Dalmatian, and a few years later it was the first British company to acquire a licence to manufacture Disney soft toys, thereby allowing many a British child to sleep alongside a plush version of Mickey Mouse or Goofy.

Disney provided many subjects for toymakers, such as Chad Valley's Snow White and the Seven Dwarves.

In the tinplate sector most of the directors of British Metal and Toy Manufacturers Ltd, originally established in 1914, survived its bankruptcy in 1921 and went on to turn out train sets, kitchen stoves and clockwork motor cars under the brand-name of Brimtoy. At the start of the 1930s Brimtoy merged with Alfred Wells, whose expansion had resulted primarily from a large

Dismal Desmond:
an example of
character
merchandising.

order from Woolworths for clockwork train sets, which he sold at 4s a dozen and which Woolworths retailed at 6d each. Throughout the 1930s Wells-Brimtoy produced some twenty new items a year, including metal pistols, prams, vehicles and humming tops. These competed for purchasers' attention with similar goods from the newly established Mettoy Company, producers, especially in its early days for Marks & Spencer, of pressed metal toys, lithographed tinplate vehicles, aeroplanes and train sets, as well as metal buildings. Capitalising on the growth in car ownership and popular interest in flying, Meccano added self-assembly planes and cars to its ranges, while Lines Brothers launched their relatively cheap range of Minic toy vehicles, along with some attractive garages.

Although most of the major tinplate companies made clockwork train sets, Frank Hornby's were generally superior in terms of quality and realism. War thwarted his intention to begin production in 1915 and it was 1921 before his first O-gauge model appeared. Versions in the liveries of the four main railway companies were soon available, all supported by massive and imaginative advertising, especially through the firm's in-house *Meccano Magazine* and the establishment in 1928 of the Hornby Railway Club along lines similar to the 1919 Meccano Guild, together with a repair service and innovative support for retailers. Hornby electric trains arrived in the mid-1920s, potentially allowing the company to capitalise on the fact that most of the four million new houses constructed in Britain between the wars were wired for electricity. Since most of these new dwellings were also relatively small, the announcement in 1938 of a smaller OO gauge was a logical step, although the outbreak of war in 1939 precluded much development. Hornby's only serious rival in the quality market, Bassett-Lowke, produced both clockwork and electric OO trains in the 1920s and its Mogul model was available in versions powered by clockwork, electricity and even steam. But the firm lacked the entrepreneurial dynamism and flair to compete commercially with Hornby, and its main profits were generated from the sale of high-quality boat models and low-cost, German-made trains distributed through Woolworths under the brand name of Trix.

Hornby's diversification into trains was more successful than some of the other new toys he marketed in the 1920s. Despite the increased use of electricity in the home, Elektron, basically a kit of electrical experiments, never really caught on, while Kemex chemistry sets were no better than those made by the market leader, E. A. Lott. From 1930 another new range, Dolly Varden metal dolls' houses and furniture, was produced specifically for girls. Meccano itself, invigorated by new colour schemes and the addition

Kliptiko and Wenebriks were two of Meccano's lesser-known competitors.

All these models made with WENEBRIK AND KLIPTIKO

of electric motors and specialised parts, such as ships' funnels, rubber tyres and hinged flat plates to facilitate greater realism, remained largely unrivalled, though plenty of foreign imitations were available, most notably the American A. C. Gilbert's Erector and Bing Brothers' Structator. Frank Hornby's main domestic competition came from William Bailey, the Birmingham-based manufacturer of grooved wooden Wenebriks and also Kliptiko, which had first appeared in 1914. Comprised of formed tubes that simply clipped together, Kliptiko required less manual dexterity than Meccano and, as the advertising made clear, was aimed at a younger age group, although the resulting models were equally skeletal. Perhaps this was why Meccano introduced Dinky Builder for younger children in 1934: with hindsight, it would have done better to have taken more notice of Minibrix, a studded rubber brick first marketed in 1935 by the Premo Rubber Company as a way of offsetting declining demand for its traditional heels and soles for shoes.

Inter-war sales of Meccano peaked in 1930 but the firm's momentum was sustained by a completely new line of small die-cast model vehicles. The technique of die-casting was an early-twentieth-century development and, like Hornby's first efforts, which appeared in 1933, used lead. The following year, however, Meccano replaced lead with a safer and more durable magnesium-zinc alloy known as mazac, and abandoned the original name of 'Modelled Miniatures' in favour of 'Dinky'. By 1938 some three hundred models were available, including saloon cars, delivery vans – often bearing advertisements for well-known products such as Hartley's jam or the *Manchester Guardian*, and, with war clouds once again gathering over Europe, a widening range of military models. Finished to very high standards and accurately modelled in detail, usually from drawings supplied by the vehicle manufacturers themselves, these die-cast toys represented a major improvement on tinplate models. They were cheap enough to make them accessible to children from all walks of life, while their small size gave them an intrinsic appeal – and not only to children: as Walter Lines observed in

HOW TO BUILD WITH

MINIBRIX

REGD. TRADE MARK

MINIBRIX reproduce in miniature almost every kind of material used by real life builders. Bricks, lintels, doors, windows, balconies, awnings, T.V. aerials—with all these any number of scale models can be built, from the simple to the elaborate. But that isn't all. With MINIBRIX you are your own architect as well as builder. What could be more satisfying than designing and building your own garage? Or making a model of your own house? The circle alongside shows how easily MINIBRIX fit together. Little pressure is needed to make the studs go into the holes — yet they hold firmly together and can be taken apart without effort.

The exclusive Minibrix interlocking device

Now see inside for details of EXTRA sets

The Minibrix studded rubber brick was perhaps the shape of things to come.

A pre-war Dinky gift set. 'Modelled Miniatures' were quickly rebranded as 'Dinky' and enjoyed enormous success.

1936, a large percentage of toys was being purchased by adults for their own use, rather than for their children.

Like Meccano, hollow-cast manufacturers also sought to diversify. After 1918 there was an understandable expectation that anti-war feeling would affect the sales of militaristic toys, and such sentiment never entirely disappeared: as late as 1932 the Dominican Republic submitted a resolution

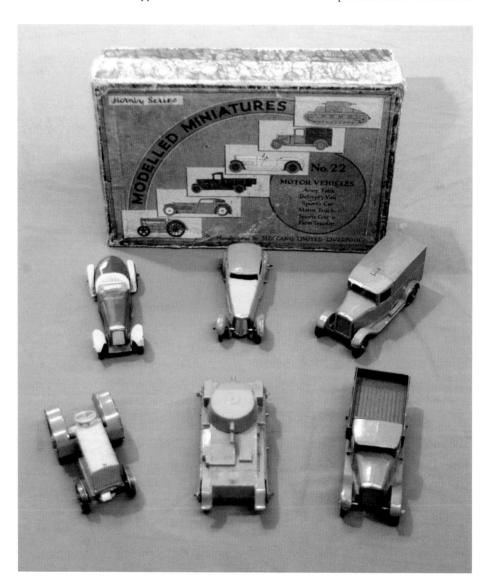

to the International Disarmament Conference calling for a global ban on the manufacture of all warlike toys. But, while Britain did have its anti-militarists, their deterrent effect was minimal. Crescent and Charbens joined the ranks of the toy-soldier manufacturers in 1922 and 1929 respectively, although both took the precaution of producing other lines as well: Charbens' figures, for example, included a window-cleaner, a costermonger and a chimpanzees' tea party. Neither firm's soldiers represented a serious challenge to William Britain, whose splendid figures continued to march off the production line in vast numbers. Equally aware of potential sensitivities, however, Britains also expanded its pre-war civilian ranges, adding well-modelled zoo and farm animals. The Home Farm series was launched in 1921 and constantly expanded throughout the inter-war period, incorporating its first die-cast farm lorry in 1934.

Models of Disney characters were produced under licence, together with souvenirs for Madame Tussaud's waxworks, and a new line, miniature gardens, appeared in 1931. By the end of the 1930s, when the firm was producing twenty million figures a year, two-thirds of them were civilians such as policemen, farm workers, railway passengers, footballers and circus performers. Their only serious pre-war competitor, John Hill & Company, also sought civilian inspiration, in particular producing some nicely modelled policemen, as well as some die-cast model cars.

Dinky models, as this letter shows, were based on actual cars.

Britains' lead figures included many non-military subjects after 1918, but soldiers, like these Highlanders, remained firm favourites.

Roberts Brothers' 'Flying Squad' game board. The dull board did not live up to the excitement promised by the title.

The police – or, more precisely, the recently formed Flying Squad – also provided the basis of a new board game launched by Roberts Brothers in 1934, one of the twenty-three games in the firm's Glevum series. Most of them had a rather dated appearance, however, and shooting gallery games of the sort produced between the wars, notably by Chad Valley and Wells-Brimtoy, probably had greater appeal to a generation of children made familiar with gunplay by the cowboy movies so frequently included in cinema matinee performances. Equally appealing were the games made by the printers Waddingtons, who began producing playing cards after the war and had great commercial success with Lexicon and Sorry in the early 1930s, as well as with cardboard jigsaws. Waddingtons' major coup, however, was to bring to Britain one of the world's most successful board games ever, Monopoly, the brainchild of the American Charles Darrow.

Although most British toys in these years continued to be made of traditional materials – G. J. Hayter started production of his long-running Victory series of wooden jigsaws in the 1930s – some makers were already beginning to turn to plastics, which offered advantages of safety, durability and lightness. Celluloid was still in use but its flammability prompted the establishment of a government committee in 1937 to examine its suitability for toys. Several years earlier, however, Palitoy, the toy division created by British Xylonite when it took over the celluloid-doll manufacturer Cascelloid, had introduced a new process to make dolls out of safer and unbreakable plastics, Bexoid and Plastex. These sold so well that Palitoy soon invested in one of the first plastic injection-moulding machines in Britain. Another early plastic, bakelite, provided the main material for Plimpton Engineering's Bayko – brick sections, windows and doors, which, slotted between upright metal rods and held together with tin ties, could be used to construct model buildings.

Lines Brothers were also moving into the new material. With public interest in flying stimulated not only by the First World War but also by the advent of commercial airlines and intense competition for the Schneider Trophy for seaplanes, Lines marketed the first toys to resemble real aeroplanes, powered by simple rubber-band motors. Made by International Model Aircraft, which was formally taken over by Lines in 1932, this FROG range – so called, it is said, because the planes Flew Right Off the Ground – proved enormously successful. Lines followed with Penguins, non-flying 1:72-scale model aircraft kits made using newly acquired plastic injection-moulding equipment. These tended, however, to be expensive because each part was moulded on a separate machine and the base material, cellulose acetate, had a tendency to warp if processed too quickly.

Another early experimentalist with plastic was Hilary Page of Kiddicraft. Trained as a child psychologist, he was concerned to design toys which young children, rather than their parents, wanted. Appreciating also that painted wooden or tin toys were potentially dangerous to infants, who tended to put everything in their mouths,

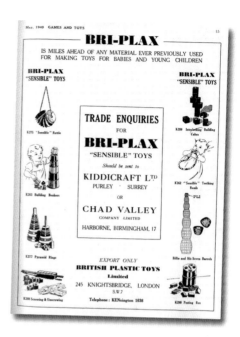

he built upon his own design experience to launch the non-flammable and colour-fast plastic Bri-Plax range in 1940. Together with the purpose-designed educational toys brought to Britain by Paul and Marjorie Abbatt from 1932 onwards, Page's toys represented another significant marker for the future, the potential of the pre-school toy sector.

Bri-Plax toys made by Hilary Page, a pioneer in plastic toys.

Children playing with bricks designed by Paul and Marjory Abbatt.

MECCANO

TOYS THAT ALL BOYS WANT

MECCANO. The most popular constructional hobby. Interchangeable parts make hundreds of realistic working models.

HORNBY-DUBLO ELECTRIC TRAINS. Accurate detail, solid construction, remote control and other features make this the most fascinating and durable of all '00' gauge systems

DINKY TOYS. Accurate metal miniatures of cars, lorries, tractors and other vehicles. Boys love to collect them!

HORNBY TRAINS. Powerful clockwork train sets and accessories for younger boys.

Made in England by Meccano Ltd., Binns Road, Liverpool 13

THE GOLDEN AGE, 1945–71

B Y CONTRAST with 1914, the outbreak of war in 1939 was no great surprise: indeed Britains had been selling boxed sets of infantry in modern battledress since the mid-1930s, while Dinky had produced an attractive (and expensive) mechanised army set. During the early months of the so-called Phoney War, toy manufacturing continued apace, with both Chad Valley and the newly established J. L. Randall benefiting in particular from the armed forces' high demand for playing cards and board games. By 1941, however, toy production had virtually ceased as both human and material resources were prioritised for the war effort. Britains and Mettoy switched to munitions, Merrythought to helmet linings and gas-mask bags; Lines Brothers' contribution included glider parts, ammunition magazines and over a million machine-guns, while Bassett-Lowke made training models for the forces, including the Mulberry harbours that proved so essential to the success of the D-Day landings in 1944.

Britain's transition to a peacetime economy after 1945 was not smooth: the country was bankrupt; physical damage had to be made good; raw materials and foodstuffs remained in short supply; and the national priorities were housing and manufactured exports. But, as in 1918, there were individuals who appreciated the business opportunities arising from the coincidence of a domestic market largely starved of new toys for several years and the widespread devastation that had engulfed two major foreign toy producers, Germany and Japan. Between 1945 and 1947 alone almost five hundred new toy businesses were established in Britain. As is the nature of all new enterprises, the majority soon disappeared into obscurity, but some were destined for success. Die-Casting Machine Tools Ltd, founded in 1940, initially produced a fully automatic zinc-alloy die-casting machine for sale to other toy manufacturers, but from 1944 it began producing its own die-cast toys under the brand name of Lone Star. In Blackpool Cherilea joined the ranks of the hollow-cast makers in 1948, and Tom Cassidy began the fancy goods business that was to develop into Casdon toys a decade later. Wendy Boston's home-made soft toys, initially sold by her unemployed husband to

Opposite: Notwithstanding this cosy advertisement in *Meccano Magazine*, all three of Meccano's main products were facing increased competition.

Bob Pelham with one of his early puppets.

a Cardiff department store, soon developed into a significant business. Made from nylon plush and with patented screw-locked eyes, her toys were at once both cuddly and safe. Further innovation came in the form of the first machine-washable bear with a quick-drying artificial filling. Long-standing friends Rodney and Leslie Smith used their demobilisation gratuities to start Lesney die-cast toys in a factory based in a disused London public house. Demobilisation money also provided the foundation capital for Dekker toys, launched in 1946 to make playsuits and Wendy houses. The following year Bob Pelham's stringed puppets appeared, initially manufactured using sawn-up ammunition cases for bodies and kitbag toggles for feet.

New businesses like these, however, were not in a position to contribute much to the ambitious export targets set for the toy industry by a government desperate to pay off massive loans incurred during and after the war. For instance, Charles Neufeld, who started making his synthetic rubber Bendy Toys in 1948, simply lacked the resources to penetrate the highly protected American market. This was where older companies had a major

A selection of Bendy Toys. Their inventor, Charles Neufeld, was one of several European refugees from Nazism who made a significant contribution to the golden age of British toy manufacture. His name was anglicised on the product.

role to play. By the time Farnell opened a new factory in 1959, 40 per cent of the firm's output was being exported, and it did particularly well in the United States. Tan-Sad was selling in more than fifty countries by the early 1950s, while the Rosebud doll factory was the largest of its type in Europe, turning out ten million dolls a year, which were exported to seventy-two countries. The major contribution came from Lines Brothers, however, and by the end of the 1950s Great Britain had become the world's largest exporter of children's toys.

At home, too, British toymakers enjoyed commercial success during the twenty-year post-war boom: personal disposable income grew by more than 2 per cent a year between 1948 and 1958, and the annual expenditure per child on toys reached £6 by 1956. Two years later total toy output was worth over £50 million a year, 90 per cent of the toys sold in Britain's shops were British-made and at thirty thousand the labour force had quadrupled since 1945.

The experience of individual firms and products was, of course, more varied. As understanding of the learning process improved, educational toys tended to do very well, building on the foundations laid by the Abbatts.

Lines Brothers contributed significantly to the post-war export drive.

A Hamley's
advertisement of
1958.

The success of an education division created in 1949 encouraged Galt to set up a toy division in 1961 and to open its own toyshops in London, Nottingham and Birmingham in 1963. One of the most successful toys of the post-war years was Denys Fisher's Spirograph, launched in 1965. By use of different-sized moveable cogs and coloured pencils, it allowed users to produce a wide range of geometric patterns and proved astonishingly attractive to children. It was voted educational toy of the year in 1965, 1966 and 1967, and was the top-selling toy in the United States in 1967.

Even more successful was Lesney, where the Smiths had been joined by Jack Odell, a gifted model-maker whose miniature of the coach used to carry Queen Elizabeth II to her coronation in 1953 inspired the hugely successful Matchbox range. Packed in small containers resembling a matchbox, more than a million of the coaches were sold, and Matchbox miniature vehicles were born. Capable of virtually indefinite expansion, the series contained seventy-five models by 1959, when four million items were sold in the United States alone. Over the next four years capital and sales both doubled, and at the end of the 1960s the firm won its fourth Queen's Export Award. In 1968 *Management Today* placed Lesney top of its list of Britain's two hundred most successful companies.

Second in the same list was Mettoy, which had relocated to Wales during the war. Continuing with many of its pre-war tinplate lines, and even adding a working stove in 1948, the company installed machines for plastic toy-making in 1948. Its most successful innovation, however, was its die-cast Corgi range, started in 1956. Often based on pioneering tie-ins with

A boy playing with a Galt train set in a Galt shop, 1965.

Spirograph cogs
and a drawing
made with them.

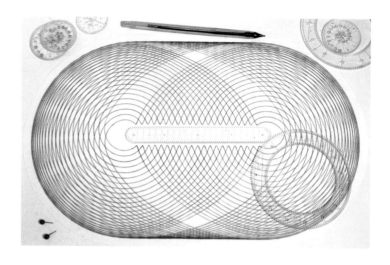

television programmes or films, these model vehicles were eminently collectable and highly innovative, being the first to incorporate windscreens and windows; fully fitted interiors followed in 1959. A series of rally cars capitalised on contemporary British success in motor sport, and the model version of the Hillman Hunter that won the London to Sydney Rally featured 'golden jacks', which allowed the wheels to be changed, and was sold complete with a plastic kangaroo. Mettoy's model of the Mini Cooper S was on the market only ten days after the real version won the Monte Carlo Rally in 1965, while another runaway winner that year, selling almost three million models, was the James Bond Aston Martin DB5, replete with gadgets such as a rising bullet-proof rear screen and a working ejector seat.

Equally impressive was the rise of Airfix, originally founded by Nicholas Kove in 1939 to make air-filled rubber toys. With Far Eastern rubber supplies

A 1960s Dinky army lorry, the design of which, apart from the addition of a driver, had advanced little from the accompanying 1930s model.

The action features on Corgi models contrasted starkly with the more staid Dinky Toys.

disrupted by the war and then by insurgency in Malaya, Kove turned instead to plastic combs. In 1948 he was commissioned to produce a promotional model of a new Massey Ferguson tractor. Because the budget was limited, he made it up in kit form and found that surplus versions sold well, not least because his injection-moulding process, using polystyrene DS and incorporating a rubber compound, resulted in a sophisticated model capable of showing the tiniest detail. His first commercial plastic kit, a model of Francis Drake's ship the *Golden Hind*, appeared in

Simply packaged, the Airfix range was cheap and extensive.

An Airfix
advertisement
in *Aeromodeller*,
1969–70.

1952. Packed in a simple polythene bag and sold for 2s through Woolworths, it proved so popular that it was produced for twenty-four hours a day for nine months. As with die-cast, the series was capable of infinite expansion, and a huge range of vehicles, ships and aircraft, both civilian and military, followed, together with boxes of HO-scale plastic figures, some larger-scale historical figures and even railway accessories.

Boxes of OO-scale
Airfix plastic
soldiers.

Airfix's success symbolised the significant shift towards the use of plastic by toy manufacturers after 1945. By 1960 plastic toys accounted for a third of all sales, and the potential of large injection-moulding machines to produce

toys capable of bearing a child's weight, thereby reducing the costs of large items and offering a viable alternative to metal and wood, drew into the industry plastics firms originally established to produce other goods. Thus Dunbee Plastics dated from 1946 but did not enter the toy sector seriously until the end of the 1950s. Following the acquisition of Combex and then of Louis Marx, the British subsidiary of Marx Inc. of New York, a manufacturer of die-cast toys in plastic and electric train sets, the new entity, Dunbee Combex Marx (DCM), soon became one of the big five of British toy manufacturing. Toy Importers Ltd, founded in 1941 and manufacturing under the brand-name of Timpo from 1942, began with wooden toys and then diversified into both die-casting and hollow-casting before turning substantially to plastics in the mid-1950s. Sharna Ware Ltd

Tom Cassidy, founder of Casdon toys, a post-war success.

Hilary Page's self-locking plastic brick, advertised in December 1948.

(1958) specialised in big wheeled plastic toys. Casdon's plastic models of household goods such as vacuum cleaners were the first toys in the world to be metallised, giving the appearance of a chrome finish. Plastic was also an obvious medium for doll-makers, though hard varieties were quickly abandoned in favour of vinyl, a more malleable and durable material. Palitoy had particular success with Tiny Tears in the 1960s. Based on an American toy, these dolls both cried and wet their nappies. It was tragic that the pre-war pioneer Hilary Page did not live to see these successes. Although he patented a studded brick made from plastic in 1947 and successfully defended it in the courts against an infringement in 1950, a similar action against Lego remained unsettled and he committed suicide in 1957. The case was not resolved in the courts until many years after his death – and then very unclearly.

Together with die-cast, plastic also allowed Britains to share in the industry's prosperity in these years. Its farm machinery series proved very popular, and in 1965 the first electric-powered model appeared – a Lister Multi-Level Elevator with the motor ingeniously hidden in a stack of hay bales. A model of the Massey Ferguson combine harvester was voted Toy of the Year by the National Association of Toy Retailers in 1978. As for the firm's traditional hollow-cast figures, the 1953 Coronation provided inspiration for a huge box of 228 figures and a die-cast coach in gold, blue and red, although its cost placed it well beyond the pocket of most families. The traditional soldiers still sold well, especially in the United States, where they had no

This hollow-cast model of Queen Elizabeth II, made by Timpo and sold for 5s 3d, was one of many items inspired by the new monarch's coronation in 1953.

Soft-toy manufacturers drew heavily on television favourites such as Andy Pandy and his friend Teddy.

serious rival, although concerns over the use of lead in children's toys represented a threat of a different sort. By the time the firm stopped using the material in 1966, it had manufactured about a thousand million lead soldiers. Some ten years earlier, and in anticipation of the lead ban, Britains had bought into a very successful plastic figure company, Herald Miniatures. One particularly innovative product, launched in 1958, was the plastic Swoppett range, a series of figures with interchangeable heads, limbs and equipment.

In soft toys, Dean's began experimenting in the 1950s with more lifelike models based on actual bears, but push-along bears, donkeys and dogs intended for younger children continued to be staple products. Merrythought took a major step forward by installing an automatic stuffing machine in 1955, although, oddly, hand stuffing was still continued. Animal pyjama cases came to feature more prominently in their production, even as their dolls became relatively less important. In any case Merrythought dolls had always been intended for younger children and had often been based on the nursery rhyme characters that provided inspiration for most soft-toy makers. Peggy Nisbet, who began her doll-making business in the early

1950s, found a ready market, especially in the United States, for her national costume and historical character dolls. Another source of ideas for new lines for dolls, soft toys – and Pelham Puppets – appeared in 1949 with the publication of the first of Enid Blyton's twenty-three books featuring appealing characters such as Noddy and Big Ears. Television also provided a stimulus for new products, and glove puppets based on the television characters Sooty and Sweep were a popular addition to Chad Valley's soft-toy range.

Soft toys apart, however, Chad Valley was beginning to struggle commercially. Its games division had benefited from the armed forces' requirements during the war, and capacity was later augmented by the purchase of Roberts Brothers' Glevum toys in 1954. Similarly, the acquisition of A. S. Cartwright Ltd in 1946 was intended to support the company's decision to branch out into tinplate. It become a public company in 1950 and enjoyed record profits in 1951, but for several years in the 1950s and again in the 1960s it was unable to pay dividends to shareholders. Tinplate was increasingly being replaced by plastic and die-cast, while Chad Valley's games appeared increasingly dated and unsophisticated, especially when compared with those of Waddingtons.

Still recognised primarily for its playing cards and jigsaws, which were acknowledged to be among the best available, Waddingtons brought out a number of best-selling games, including Cluedo in 1949. In one sense the concept behind Cluedo was rather old-fashioned – characters who could only have come from a 1930s novel moving through the rooms of a large rambling country house in an effort to identify the killer of the unfortunate Dr Black, together with the weapon used and the location of the crime. But with attractively printed cards and playing board, together with moulded playing pieces and nicely modelled miniature weapons, the game's physical presentation was thoroughly modern and proved highly attractive. The same was true of Waddingtons' Buccaneer, a revamped pre-war game, and Blast-Off, a 1969 game inspired, like a growing number of toys, by the contemporary space race.

Chad Valley was not the only company to experience difficulties in the favourable post-war years. After peaking in 1956, Meccano's profitability fell away so severely that by the early

Waddingtons' games, such as Buccaneer, were attractively presented.

THE MECCANO MAGAZINE   xxiii

BUCCANEER IS BACK!

"BUCCANEER"

one of the most popular and well loved of pre-war board games, is, as its name implies, a swashbuckling, adventurous game full of interest, fun, and ingenuity. Produced to Waddington's own standards of high quality, "Buccaneer" contains all the thrills of voyages to Treasure Island, and bringing home the treasure . . . including realistic looking diamonds, rubies, bars of gold, pearls, and barrels of rum! Equally valuable cargoes can be captured on the High Seas . . . or you can trade for cargo at a foreign port.

FOR 2 TO 6 PLAYERS

25/-

(Including Purchase Tax)

Published by

JOHN WADDINGTON LIMITED

40 WAKEFIELD ROAD, LEEDS 10.   Phone : Leeds 72244
London Office : 43 Hertford Street, W.1.   Phone : GRO 8701

1960s the company was in serious deficit. The basic construction set, substantially unchanged for thirty years, was adjudged by *Which?* magazine in 1964 to be complicated, not very versatile and poorly packaged. Bayko, which Meccano had acquired in 1949, scored equally poorly and had not been marketed very vigorously. In the wings lurked the threat of a more flexible, less complex construction toy based on studded plastic bricks, and sold in Britain from 1959 by British Lego.

Meccano's Dinky range also faced intensifying competition. Crescent's success with a well-timed range of Grand Prix racing cars was one thing, but far more serious was the way in which Dinky was being left behind by both the cheaper

Unchanged for thirty years – a Meccano advertisement of 1958.

Meccano never marketed Bayko with sufficient vigour.

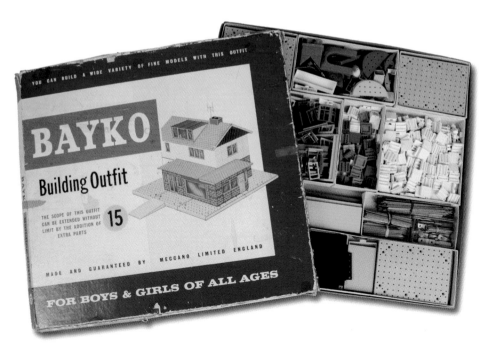

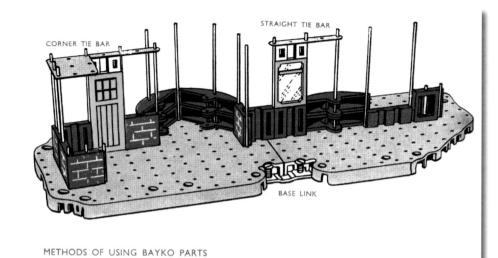

CORNER TIE BAR

STRAIGHT TIE BAR

BASE LINK

METHODS OF USING BAYKO PARTS

Like Meccano itself, Bayko required literate and dexterous users.

Lego proved more appealing than either Meccano or Bayko.

Matchbox range and by the more sophisticated models produced by Corgi. Competition became even stiffer when Lines Brothers introduced Spot On die-cast vehicles in 1959, followed a year later by a range from Lone Star, hitherto best-known primarily for its huge variety of die-cast cap-firing guns. Matters were not helped when Meccano's managing director turned down a proposal for a revolutionary low-friction wheel/axle assembly to improve the running of model vehicles. Subsequently the American

Dinky Supertoys were attractive but expensive.

Meccano's joint managing director, Roland Hornby, tried in vain to reassure his shareholders at the 1963 annual general meeting.

> The decision of a majority of the Board to alter the original proposal to give one vote for each share has brought some adverse and inaccurate comment in the Press.
>
> I wish to state that no take-over talks have taken place at any time, and there has never been any disagreement amongst my family.
>
> I feel that the steps we are now contemplating will place our "A" Ordinary Shareholders in a better position than those of many Companies where no enfranchisement of any kind has been made in respect of non-voting shares.

manufacturer Mattel incorporated this new technology in its Hot Wheels models in 1968, with devastating impact on all British die-cast makers. Meccano also faced growing competition in the train-set market as Woolworths began selling French-made Playcraft sets and Lines came out with Tri-ang railways. Both were sold through a much larger number of outlets than Hornby trains, whose availability was restricted to a limited number of franchised dealers. Both used more plastic than metal in their models, which were thus cheaper, and, if Hornby products remained technically superior, their reputation with customers and retailers suffered badly in a debacle over supplies when the old three-rail running system was changed to two in 1959. Five years later Frank Hornby's son Roland was effectively forced to resign as managing director, and Meccano, by now widely referred to in the trade press as 'the sick man of the industry', was sold to Lines Brothers. Some modernisation of Meccano construction sets followed, and among the new products added (under licence) to Meccano's portfolio was Play Doh, the first modelling material to present a serious challenge to Harbutt's Plasticine.

The Merton factory of Lines Brothers, the largest toy concern in the world in the 1950s.

The purchase of Meccano by the Lines Group, long the dominant force in the British toy industry, was the latest in a seemingly endless series of acquisitions that enabled the firm to widen its product base away from its familiar and successful ranges of wheeled toys, wooden dolls' houses, Minic tinplate and soft toys. By the mid-1950s Lines had nine factories in Britain and another ten in Canada, Australia, New Zealand and South Africa. As before the war, the strategy was to buy up three types of company: those, like Rovex Plastics (bought in 1951), with specialised production facilities; those, like Meccano, with well-known brands in need of modernisation; and those with a particular product that needed the development and selling expertise that a large enterprise like Lines could provide. For this reason P. A. Adolph allowed Lines to acquire a stake in his table football game, Subbuteo, which enjoyed considerable success in the aftermath of England's victory in the 1966 football World Cup. Minimodels, makers of the Scalextric slot car racing system, benefited in similar fashion. Within two years of buying the firm in 1958, Lines had replaced the existing tinplate cars with plastic ones and added variable speed controllers. The original rubber track sections, which simply clipped together, gave way in 1963 to lockable plastic sections, and the realism of the race track was further enhanced by the addition of some attractive buildings.

In other sectors, however, Lines increasingly seemed to be imitating the best-selling toys of other makers. In essence, only their generally higher price and more consistent use of a standard scale distinguished the Spot On range from other companies' die-cast products, while the introduction of Tri-ang

Rovex trains, eventually acquired by Lines.

railways merely added another competitor to an already overcrowded market. Not surprisingly, the acquisition of Meccano was quickly followed by product rationalisation, with Lines abandoning its die-cast range in favour of Dinky and merging its own train-set system with Hornby under the brand name of Tri-ang-Hornby. Another, arguably more successful imitation was the Sindy doll, produced from 1962 by the Lines subsidiary Pedigree. Fundamentally Sindy was a copy of Mattel's Barbie, albeit initially modelled on an adolescent girl rather than a mature woman, but clearly designed to appeal to an older age group than traditional dolls. Accordingly, Sindy was provided with a new outfit every six months, and her available accessories eventually included a kitchen, a bedroom, a bath, a pony and a battery-operated scooter.

Two famous names came together when Hornby and Tri-ang railways were merged.

Meccano—Triang Get-together

FOR many years, two model railway systems existed side by side. To some extent each duplicated the equipment of the other. They were both very good systems; each one had its own unique features but at the same time there were many similarities and some duplication of equipment. Well, as you all know by now, the two railways were Hornby Dublo and Triang Railways and they are now united to form the Triang Hornby line, which incorporates many of the best features of each of the two earlier systems. Not only does this amalgamation provide an unequalled potential for development and expansion, but it removes one of the newcomer's greatest headaches—which one to choose! And the happiest thing about it is that everyone wins, for the new system is undoubtedly the best in the world.

Similar problems of choice have existed in the magazine field. Our own Meccano Magazine and the newer Triang Magazine inevitably appealed to the same readers, and the choice between the two—which one to buy—must have been very difficult.

As from last month, Triang Magazine ceased publication, and this means that, as with the two railway systems, there is now one BIG monthly hobby journal—The Meccano Magazine. You can still join the Triang Club, with its colourful badge and membership card and more details of this will be found on page 23. Another unique result of this get-together is the magnificent double-page spread Picture-Story feature on the Saturn Moon Rocket on pages 24-25. These thrilling drawings have been one of the most popular features of Triang Magazine.

Meccano Magazine put a positive spin on the Lines takeover.

Lines failed in a bid to secure production rights from Hasbro for Action Man, the boys' equivalent of Sindy, and also based on an American toy, GI Joe. As it was, Palitoy secured these rights and enjoyed considerable success from 1964 with a range of figures and accessories. So popular did these figures become, particularly a skydiver and Superman, that by the 1970s it was estimated that there was one Action Man in Britain for every boy.

A display of Palitoy Action Men at the 1966 British Toy Fair.

THE END?

FROM THE mid-1960s the circumstances that had so favoured Britain's domestic toymakers began to deteriorate. By now both Germany and Japan had fully recovered from the war and their toy industries were competing for markets, as also were American manufacturers. This coincided with a liberalisation of international trade, which opened up Britain's markets to foreign competition by dismantling protective tariffs and import controls. Things got even tougher in the 1970s as huge rises in oil prices not only drove up the price of plastics, by now the industry's major manufacturing material, but also generated unprecedentedly high levels of domestic price inflation and soaring interest rates, which at one point reached 17 per cent. At the same time British toy exports were made less competitive by rising labour costs and the high value of sterling.

One response was a renewed effort by the trade to spread toy-buying more evenly over the whole year. Individual firms sought refuge in diversification or organisational change. Chad Valley became Britain's largest soft-toy maker when it purchased Chiltern Toys in 1967, while Denys Fisher bought up Wendy Boston and Hayter's jigsaws went to J. W. Spear. Wells-Brimtoy, whose tin toys were particularly hard hit by Japanese imports, amalgamated in 1970 with Keithe Lowe, a manufacturer of pressed tubular-steel toys. Peggy Nisbet's business was bought by a Canadian investment company in 1975. But these were merely ripples in the pond compared with the tidal wave created by the sinking and break-up of Lines Brothers in 1971. With thirty-nine separate manufacturing units, the group's production costs were unsustainable in an increasingly competitive market, especially as exports were too heavily dependent on distant and relatively small Commonwealth markets. Nor did it adjust well to the challenge of mail-order sales, a method which allowed Sharna Ware to capture a significant portion of Lines' existing three-quarter share of the market for large wheeled toys. Contemporary opinion was that Lines had outgrown its own managerial competence, a credible view perhaps, given that most parts of the dismembered group were rapidly snapped up by new owners and made

Opposite:
A century after the birth of the British toy industry, a British girl sits surrounded by toys, most of them bearing the names of international manufacturers, and most actually made in the Far East.

profitable. Airfix bought Meccano and Tri-ang Pedigree; DCM acquired Rovex-Tri-ang; and the American corporation Milton Bradley acquired 74 per cent of the equity in Arrow Games. Tri-ang itself went to Barclay Securities, which in quick succession also bought other strugglers such as Sebel, Chad Valley and Chiltern, rationalised production, and then sold off many of the assets, including the old Lines site at Merton, before quitting the toy business in 1973 as suddenly as it had entered it.

By this time the economic climate for Britain's toymakers was becoming even worse. Toy sales fell in real terms by 10 per cent between 1974 and 1976, while the average return on capital paid by the twelve leading companies fell by more than half between 1976 and 1979. Some firms, such as Pelham Puppets, survived by laying off workers, but a persistent trickle of company failures turned into a torrent after 1979 as almost all of the major firms collapsed. Meccano was the first to go, closing its factory gates in November 1979 on a workforce and a management equally resistant to the changes demanded by Airfix to make the company's operations more cost-effective. A few months later dealing in DCM shares, which had once stood at 200p, was suspended when they fell to 22p, and the receivers were called in. The same fate befell Airfix in January 1981 when half-year losses of £2.3 million were projected. Five months later Lesney, whose Superfast range had allowed it to fight back against the challenge of Hot Wheels to record profits of £10 million as recently as 1976, also went into receivership, its shares suspended at 11p. In 1982 it was the turn of Berwick Timpo, when losses of £1.7 million were massively increased by the discovery of a hitherto unsuspected £600,000 deficit. With its closure, total employment in British toy manufacturing had fallen to 24,500, compared with 42,500 in 1979, but the storm was still not over. In 1983 Lone Star went down and Mettoy also found itself in the hands of receivers, unable to withstand cumulative losses of more than £8 million in three years to September 1982. Pedigree stopped trading in 1986, by which time corporate membership of the British Toy Manufacturers Association, which stood at 444 in 1978, was down to about 260.

The causes of this spectacular collapse were complex. The difficult economic environment certainly played a part, affecting British manufacturers more severely than their international counterparts because intensified competition exposed underlying weaknesses that had gone largely unaddressed in easier times. These included poor packaging, inefficient production and amateurish sales techniques. In particular, British firms were slow to exploit the advertising potential of commercial television – surprising in view of their willingness to draw on television as a source of ideas for product lines. Meccano, for example, produced a model of Thunderbird 2 with spring-loaded legs and *Star Trek* vessels that fired plastic discs. Mettoy

sold about three million models of its Batmobile. But it was different when it came to advertising. Lesney's success bred such complacency, for example, that in 1968 its total advertising budget was only £10,000, compared with some £240,000 spent by Mattel on British television alone.

The deserted Meccano factory, a symbol of the decline of British toy manufacture.

It also seems that, in a market environment more competitive than at any time since the 1920s, British managers were simply not up to the task of running large enterprises. Neither Lines Brothers nor Airfix was able to break down managerial complacency and workforce conservatism at Meccano, while other firms simply made bad strategic decisions. Mettoy's ill-fated diversification into computers was compounded by its decision to ignore the microchip revolution, which was rapidly carrying American and Japanese toymakers to the top of the bestsellers' list. Berwick Timpo did diversify but its child guidance range did not do well. Meccano was so bereft of inspiration that its only major innovation in the 1970s was a range of large pressed-steel vehicles under the name 'Mogul', which was nothing more than a dearer imitation of the market leader, Tonka. For DCM and Lesney, acquisitions in the United States proved costly mistakes, so much so in DCM's case that by 1979 its liabilities there exceeded its assets by $12 million.

Whatever the causes of the collapse, its effect was to rip the heart out of British toy manufacturing. Independent specialist toy retailers fared little better. Their difficulties had in effect begun in 1964, when the abolition of retail price maintenance allowed large retail organisations and mail-order firms to undercut them on price, thereby reducing their market share to only 27 per cent by 1982. While bulk-buying chains such as Toymaster appeared to offer some protection, even this came under threat from Toys R Us, which had thirty-three branches in Britain by 1991, each one, it was calculated, resulting in the closure of eight independents. Not surprisingly, the number of independent retailers fell between 1980 and 1984 alone from five thousand to 3,800, and by 1991 their market share was down to just 12 per cent.

Toys R Us was the retail manifestation of the substantial international takeover of the British toy business that followed the manufacturing collapse of the early 1980s. American makers, in particular, had long been seeking to establish themselves in Britain: Mattel, for example, purchased the doll-maker Rosebud, and General Mills bought Denys Fisher and, in 1968, Palitoy. Such was the demise of British manufacturing capacity that Palitoy alone accounted for 10 per cent of toy sales in Britain in 1984; within a year or so, however, even this famous brand-name disappeared when General Mills sold the firm to another American corporation, Kenner Parker.

Of course, some bucked the trend. The makers of the highly successful Mastermind game, Invicta Plastics, won a Queen's Export Award in 1978. Dekker's playsuits and Wendy houses continued to do well, as did educational and nursery toy producers such as Chelful, Sharna and Casdon, although the last moved its manufacturing facilities to China at the end of the decade. There was even a significant newcomer in this sector in 1980 when Torquil Norman, a former director of DCM, established Bluebird Toys. His numerous successes included a yellow teapot house, which broke away from the traditional dolls' house format. In the course of the 1990s, however, Bluebird was sold to Mattel, adding to the seemingly endless attrition of famous British toymakers and brand-names.

Even when the names survived, they often bore little relationship to the significant manufacturing enterprises that once produced them. Thus Meccano production was first consolidated in France by General Mills before the product was sold to the Japanese Nikko Group in 2000. General Mills also sold Airfix to Humbrol, manufacturer of the paints often used by Airfix model-makers. After Humbrol went bankrupt, Airfix was purchased by Hornby in 2007. Hornby itself survived the collapse of its Airfix parent company by means of a management buy-out, though production of its trains was soon transferred to China. A management buy-out also initially allowed the Dean's brand to survive, although the original Dean's Rag Book Company soon went out of existence. Similarly, Pelham Puppets have been resurrected, but the original company went through several changes of ownership after the founder's death in 1980, before disappearing in 1993. Corgi was sold to Mattel in 1986 and underwent a management buy-out in 1995 which established Corgi Classics, a firm that, after a further period of American ownership, was purchased by Hornby in 2008. Matchbox and Dinky were initially acquired by the Hong Kong-based group Universal Holdings, the former eventually passing to Mattel in 1997.

Even those firms that survived the worst of the 1980s crash did not always retain their independence, Waddingtons going to Hasbro, while Britains, which passed through several hands following its initial sale to the Dobson Park Group in 1984, was also eventually acquired by American owners. Chad Valley, which had been taken over by Palitoy in 1978, was acquired by Woolworths ten years later. When Woolworths itself went bankrupt, Chad Valley passed to the Home Retail Group, parent company of Argos, which is today the exclusive supplier of this famous brand.

Over the course of little more than a hundred years British toy-making turned full circle. The golden age of the specialist retailers came and largely went. The great brand-names associated with the golden age of manufacturing may remain, but they are mostly foreign-owned and the products are mostly made abroad. By the end of the twentieth century almost three-quarters of the toys being sold in the domestic British market, worth about a billion pounds a year, were foreign-made and a fifth of all toy imports came from one country – China. Sadly, there was more than a hint of truth in the observation of one journalist in 1994 that 'all that remains of the once flourishing British toy industry seems to be board games, self-tying shoelaces and hollow imitation vacuum cleaners and lawn mowers'.

PLACES TO VISIT

The Bear Museum, 38 Dragon Street, Petersfield, Hampshire GU13 4JJ.
   Telephone: 01730 265108.
   Website: www.bearmuseum.co.uk
Beaumaris Museum of Childhood Memories, 1 Castle Street, Beaumaris,
   Anglesey LL58 8AP. Telephone: 01248 810448.
   Website: www.beaumaris.org.uk/chmuseum.html
Bethnal Green Museum of Childhood, Cambridge Heath Road, London E2
   9PA. Telephone: 020 8983 5200. (The museum holds a very wide
   selection of material from British toy manufacturers.)
   Website: www.museumofchildhood.org.uk
Brighton Toy and Model Museum, 52–55 Trafalgar Street, Brighton BN1 4EB.
   Telephone: 01273 749494.
   Website: www.brightontoymuseum.co.uk
Childhood Memories Toy Museum, The Palace Building, Grand Parade,
   Tynemouth, Tyne and Wear NE30 4JH. Telephone: 0191 259 1776.
   Website: www.tynemouthtoymuseum.co.uk

Edinburgh Museum of Childhood, 42 High Street, Edinburgh EH1 1TG.
Telephone: 0131 529 4142.
Website: www.scotland.com/museums/museum-childhood
House on the Hill Toy Museum, 12 Grove Hill, Stansted Mountfitchet, Essex
CM24 8SP. Telephone: 01279 813237.
Website: www.stanstedtoymuseum.com
Ilkley Toy Museum, Whitton Croft Road, Ilkley, West Yorkshire LS29 9HR.
Telephone: 01943 603855. Website: www.ilkleytoymuseum.co.uk
Lilliput Museum of Antique Dolls and Toys, High Street, Brading, Isle of Wight
PO36 0DJ. Telephone: 01983 407231.
Website: www.lilliputmuseum.org.uk
Pollock's Toy Museum, 1 Scala Street, London W1P 1LT.
Telephone: 020 7636 3452. Website: www.pollockstoymuseum.com
Sudbury Hall and the National Trust Museum of Childhood, Sudbury,
Ashbourne, Derbyshire DE6 5HT. Telephone: 01283 585305.
Website: www.nationaltrust.org.uk/sudburyhall/
The Teddy Bear Museum, 240 Broadway, Wimbledon, London SW19 1SB.
Telephone: 020 8545 8320. Website: www.polkatheatre.com
Toys of Yesteryear, Barton Marina, Barton-under-Needwood, Staffordshire
DE13 8DZ. Telephone: 01283 712770.
Website: www.toysofyesteryear.co.uk
Vina Cooke Museum of Dolls and Bygone Childhood, The Old Rectory,
Cromwell, Newark, Nottinghamshire NG23 6JE.
Telephone: 01636 821364. Website: www.vinadolls.co.uk
West Wales Museum of Childhood, Pen-ffynon, Llangeler, Carmarthenshire
SA44 5EY. Telephone: 01559 370428.
Website: www.toymuseum.wales.co.uk
Whitby Museum, Pannett Park, Whitby, North Yorkshire YO21 1RE.
Telephone: 01947 602908. Website: www.whitbymuseum.org.uk

FURTHER READING

For works which discuss the general development of the industry or
specific companies and manufacturers, see:

Bassett-Lowke, Jane. *Bassett-Lowke*. Rail Romances, 1999.
Brown, Kenneth D. *The British Toy Business. A History since 1700*. Hambledon, 1996.
Brown, Kenneth D. *Factory of Dreams. A History of Meccano Limited*. Carnegie
Press, 2008.
Brown, Kenneth D. 'Models in History: a Micro-Study of Late Nineteenth-
Century British Entrepreneurship', *Economic History Review*, XLII
(1989), pp. 528–537.

Brown, Kenneth D. 'The Collapse of the British Toy Industry, 1979–1984',
    Economic History Review, XLVI (1993), pp. 592–606.
Brown, Kenneth D. 'Family Failure? Lines Brothers, Deceased 1971', in
    J. Astrachan (editor), *Family Business Casebook Annual* (2005), pp. 81–100.
Fawdry, Marguerite. *British Tin Toys*. New Cavendish, 1990.
Fuller, Roland. *The Bassett-Lowke Story*. New Cavendish, 1982.
Garrett, John. *World Encyclopaedia of Model Soldiers*. New Cavendish, 1981.
Lines, Walter. *Looking Backwards and Looking Forwards*. Privately published, 1958.
McReavy, Anthony. *Toy Story. The Life and Times of Inventor Frank Hornby*.
    Ebury Press, 2002.
Nisbet, Peggy. *The Peggy Nisbet Story*. Hobby House Press, 1988.

There are numerous publications dealing with the best-known British toys
and among the most useful for details of the relevant manufacturing
companies are:

Axe, John. *The Magic of Merrythought*. Hobby House Press, 1986.
Foster, Michael. *History of Hornby-Dublo Trains, 1939–1964*. New
    Cavendish, 1980.
Hammond, Pat. *Tri-ang Railways. The Story of Rovex*, volume 1, 1950–1964.
    New Cavendish, 1993.
Hammond, Pat. *Tr-iang Hornby. The Story of Rovex*, volume 2, 1965–1971.
    New Cavendish, 1998.
Hammond, Pat. *Hornby Railways. The Story of Rovex*, volume 3, 1972–1996.
    New Cavendish, 2005.
Leech, David. *Pelham Puppets. A Collector's Guide*. Crowood Press, 2008.
Lines, Richard, and Hellstrom, Leif. *Frog Model Aircraft, 1932–1976*. New
    Cavendish, 1989.
Mansell, Colette. *Collectors' Guide to British Dolls since 1920*. Robert Hale, 1983.
Mansell, Colette. *The History of Sindy: Britain's Top Teenage Doll*, 1962–1994.
    New Cavendish, 2006.
Opie, James. *The Great Book of Britains*. New Cavendish, 1993.
Ramsay, John. *British Diecast Model Toys Catalogue*. Swapmeet, 1995.
Ward, Arthur. *Airfix – Celebrating 50 Years of the Greatest Plastic Kits in the
    World*. Harper Collins, 2003.
Ward, Arthur. *The Boys' Book of Airfix*. Ebury Press, 2009.

Works quoted in the text:
Benedetta, M. *The Street Markets of London*. John Miles,1936.
Lansley, Hubert. *My Meccano Days*. Constructor Quarterly, 1994.
Roberts, Robert. *A Ragged Schooling*. Fontana, 1978.
Wells, H. G. *The New Machiavelli*. Penguin, 1970.

INDEX